Divine
Intervention

———◆———

*A Tragic Memoir
of Unwavering Faith*

GUNMOLLY KODIAD

DIVINE INTERVENTION
A TRAGIC MEMOIR OF UNWAVERING FAITH

iUniverse books may be ordered through booksellers or by contacting:

iUniverse
1663 Liberty Drive
Bloomington, IN 47403
www.iuniverse.com
844-349-9409

ISBN: 978-1-6632-2733-1 (sc)
ISBN: 978-1-6632-2734-8 (hc)
ISBN: 978-1-6632-2732-4 (e)

Library of Congress Control Number: 2021916936

Print information available on the last page.

iUniverse rev. date: 08/18/2021

*To my youngest daughter, Brayly; it is the love I have
for you that has made this father go above and beyond
and seek answers no one else could provide*

CONTENTS

1
CHAPTER

◆

What Were You Thinking?

WHAT WERE YOU THINKING?

That was a comical question, as the fifth hour had passed. The view was tremendous, sitting on the edge of the office building located at 1920 E. Hallandale Beach Blvd. I remember waking up at my marble hotel / condominium convinced today was the day. And I was pissed that the cord on my blow-dryer was too short to electrocute myself in the bathtub. No matter how hard I tried, I just couldn't plunge the screwdriver deep enough into my heart to make a difference. I was forced to head to the office. I was absolutely convinced that the minute I left the condo, I would be swept off my feet by the FBI. In my mind—or what was left of it—I was public enemy number one. Yet to this day, what crime had I committed?

My general decline had started about sixteen months earlier when I'd decided I wanted to get my family out of South Florida because my prize possession was getting ready to leave the safety of her middle school and enter high school in Broward County,

Florida. That would be my only child, Amanda. No way. No how. We were heading north to the safety of a small town in the middle of the mountains, none other than Jasper, Georgia. Little did I know that Jasper was the methamphetamine mecca of the state of Georgia.

We took the proceeds from the sale of our home in Sunny Ranches, Florida, $897,000, and built an eight thousand-square foot mountain home on three acres with a roaring stream. We had made it out of the hustle and bustle and drugs of South Florida and into the safety and security of mountain living, where the only care in the world was, Will we see a black bear on the way to school in the morning?

My general decline started because I knew it would take time to close my medical practice. So I moved my daughter, mother-in-law, and ex-wife to Jasper in 2005, and I purchased a hotel condo in Hallandale, directly across the street from my office in Hallandale Beach Florida. I would spend a week in Florida and then a week in Georgia while closing the practice and then eventually rejoin the family full-time in Georgia.

2
CHAPTER

◆

The Day I Dreaded the Most

WE LOADED THE MOBILE HOME WITH MY EX-WIFE, KAREN; Amanda; three large parrots; and two cats and headed to the mountains, saying goodbye to South Florida, at least for the girls, for the last time. I was to spend a couple of days there and then drive back to Florida, sell the mobile home, and catch up on lost patients and mounds of paperwork.

Saying goodbye to my daughter was the hardest thing I'd ever had to do in my life. I must have lost ten pounds in tears from the mountain home until I hit Atlanta.

I knew it would only be a week before I would see Amanda again, but this thought of doom was always there. What if, God forbid, something happened and I couldn't get to her in time? I just could not live with that.

One of the conditions of making this move was that my mother-in-law had to make the trip and move in with us. My mind needed to have the security of a backup plan to protect my daughter. If something was ever to happen to Karen when I was in Florida, my mother-in-law, Donna, was there just in case.

3
CHAPTER

◆

My Biggest Fear Realized

A FEW MONTHS HAD GONE BUY, AND THE GIRLS WERE settling in. summer was ending. Amanda was about the start a new school. She was to enter eighth grade in a small country town with a population of about twenty-five thousand back then. I ate every fingernail off to the bone wondering how her first day of school had gone, and my worst fears were realized.

I picked my daughter up, and I asked how her first day had gone. In my mind, I heard, "Oh, Daddy, I loved it." What came out was, "I hate it here. Today was the worst day of my life. Can we please move back to Florida?"

My heart shattered into a thousand pieces. Everything I had done in my life to protect my Amanda had just gone down the tubes. And two new words were introduced in my psyche—*depression* and *anxiety.*

4
CHAPTER

◆

What the Hell is Wrong with My Legs?

S OMETHING WAS VERY WRONG WITH ME STARTING ABOUT June 2007. By this time, the girls had been in the mountains about a year and had made new friends. Amanda and Karen were adjusting, but I was having a tough go of it. I kept a small Honda at the parking place in Atlanta. I would fly in the five days and work on the new house and property.

By this time, Amanda, was fourteen to fifteen and had her fist boyfriend. Matthew gave me comfort. He was a polite, well-raised Georgia gentleman. I felt good knowing he was looking after my Amanda when I was in Florida. Matthew took a great deal of stress off my mind. I am indebted to that young man.

Going back ten years before moving to Georgia, my relationship with my ex-wife, Karen, was good but definitely not the norm. I always classified it as two ships crossing in the night. She was a cheerleading coach and stay-at-home mother. She liked to stay up until 2:00 a.m. doing God knows what on the computer and sleep until noon. I would go to bed shortly after work around 9:00 p.m. and leave the house at 6:00 a.m. We coexisted and would meet in the middle on occasion.

The truth of the matter is I was very unhappy and had fallen out of love a long time ago. But my career as the owner of a trauma-based orthotic/prosthetic facility meant my average day was 6:00 a.m. until 8:00 p.m. five days a week, on call twenty-four seven, which meant always seeing hospital patients on weekends.

No matter how miserable I was, though, even though it might have been only for thirty minutes a day, I vowed a day would never go by that I would not hug my Amanda.

5
CHAPTER

◆

Daddy, Stay

B OY, OH BOY, DID I SCREW UP. I FAILED FATHERING 101—*BIG-time*! Amanda was just a wee bit over two years old, and she had just graduated to her big girl bed. I had turned the lock on her door the other way around so she could not leave her room in the middle of the night. Hell, we had a pool and a pond. I was overprotective of my baby girl. That practice is probably considered child abuse now. Arrest me. Who cares? I'd been through hell and back as a frequent flyer.

Back to Amanda and her first night in her big girl bed. My ex and I were so excited. We put her to bed and walked outside to peek through her bedroom window to see how she was doing. She was so damn cute; she just sat up in the middle of her bed for about two minutes looking around. The wife and I looked at each other; high-fived; and said, "We got this!"

Then it happened. Amanda went to the bedroom door and started knocking on the door and screaming at the top of her lungs.

My ex and I were brave. We agreed to let her scream it out.

Three seconds later, big brave daddy caved and went in. I decided I would lie down with her until she fell asleep.

Once Amanda was asleep, I started to sneak out. And that's when it happened—the words that would forever change my life for the next fourteen years. "Daddy, *stay*."

Daddy stayed and stayed and stayed. And for the next fourteen years, Amanda would not go to bed without Daddy lying with her until she fell asleep. Some nights it would be fifteen minutes; most nights, it was much longer. A lot of things were lost that night, mostly my sex life.

That was an audible I made. It was the worst call in the history of calls, and it greatly affected mine and Karen's marriage. Well, at least it did to me. I vowed that night I would always be faithful to Karen, as this was my dumb-ass decision.

Back to the statement about our marriage being like two ships passing in the night. It literally was, more so than ever. The downfall of this marriage was 100 percent my fault.

6
CHAPTER

◆

What is in the Water in Georgia? Everyone is Getting Divorced

A FEW MONTHS AFTER WE HAD MOVED TO GEORGIA, MY wife had met two southern girls, one named Tammy the other named Kanyon. They were both cheer and dance coaches, and it was a perfect fit. Remember, my ex-wife Karen was a cheer coach. Tammy was a wiry-looking thing with a loud mouth and honestly was just quite obnoxious.

There was something about Kanyon. I remember the first time I saw her. If you were to ask me what I had for breakfast this morning I could not tell you, but I can recall every little detail about Kanyon the day I met her. She was not supermodel material; believe you me. Kanyon was very simple and plain. She was wearing a yellow T-shirt and blue shorts. Her hair was a mess. She was holding a baby named Brayly, who was probably about one years old.

To the day I die, the one thing that hit me the most was the look on Kanyon's face. She was very quiet. We didn't say a word to each other. I merely glimpsed at her for maybe five seconds, but that five seconds would have an impact on me that I just to this day *can't* explain. Kanyon had this look on her sweet face that told me she had the weight of the world on her shoulders. I couldn't understand how someone so young could harbor such inner anguish.

She didn't know it, and frankly, neither did I. But we were meant to meet. We connected at that moment in the biggest of ways! More about Kanyon later.

7
CHAPTER

◆

What's Wrong with Me?

IT WAS NOW APPROXIMATELY SUMMER 2007, AND I WAS physically spent. I *couldn't* sleep to save my life. The hotel/condo I purchased was convenient, as it was located across the street from my office. But because it was a hotel/condo, guests were checking in at all hours of the morning, and car alarms were constantly going off. The hallways were full of noise and drunks.

When I was back in Florida, my days were hell on earth. Each and every day was eighteen hours plus. I had mounds of paperwork to catch up on. I had patients to see. I was physically and psychologically spent. My partner, Jason, was doing everything in his power to hold down the fort. I had a staff of twelve telling me I was losing clients daily because, even though they were handling things, there were certain physicians who were simply used to sending their patients our way. I was an orthotist, the son of Alphonso, need I say more. I was excellent at what I did. Alphonso was my dad, and he was one of the finest orthopedic surgeons South Florida had ever seen.

He was the go-to guy from, I would say, the mid 1970s until 2010. He was Italian and damn good-looking, and he knew it. I always referred to Dad as King Midas. Everything the man touched turned to gold, whether it was real estate, jade, oil paintings, ivory, or wine. If Dad took the time to get involved in it, he became an authority on the subject and made money. He was a brilliant orthopedic surgeon and diagnostician.

My father was admired by the insurance companies because he was *honest* to a T. If you were full of shit, he told the insurance companies to give their client zilch. If you were truly injured, my father told the insurance company to pay the man. He never disrespected the oath he swore to uphold. He was like Perry Mason in court, and the lawyers who had him on their side flaunted him like a proud peacock. When the lawyers on the other side knew he was involved in their case, their butt holes puckered.

I was an excellent and honest practitioner because I started my career working for my dad as his cast room tech.

He had passed now, and I missed him terribly. But I'd picked up a few things along the way. Dad was a great provider, but he lacked in certain areas when it came to family. We will touch on that subject briefly a bit later.

8
CHAPTER

◆

Praying for Lyme Disease

I COULDN'T SLEEP. ON ANY GIVEN DAY, MY WEIGHT HELD AT 210 pounds or dropped 185 pounds. My legs feel like insects were crawling on them. Something was wrong. I was getting very depressed. I missed Amanda so much when I was in Florida, and I felt like I was missing her growing up. This concern was compounded by the fact that she had her first boyfriend, Matthew, along with a boatload of new friends; was 772 miles away from me; and never called.

I kept telling myself that maybe—since, when I was in Georgia, I was constantly clearing my property—I'd been bitten by a tick and had contracted Lyme disease. I was praying I had Lyme disease; if it wasn't that, then I knew I was losing my mind.

I made an appointment to get a full workup from the family internal medicine doctor—blood work, urinalysis, stress test, and carotid ultrasound.

9
CHAPTER

◆

The Results are In

THE RESULTS WERE IN, AND I'D SCORED 100 PERCENT. ALL the lab work was perfect. My doctor told me my urine was so clean that, if for whatever reason, I had to drink my urine, chugalug; it was that pure. I was devastated, because now I knew I needed to see a psychiatrist.

I decided to see a shrink over by Avana Hospital. His name escapes me, although it should not, because this man was almost responsible for my death and the deaths of others. I told him what was going on, and he prescribed Prozac and told me to return in two weeks. The shrink told me that these meds could lead to thoughts of suicide and could take weeks to begin to work.

In my mind, or what was left of it, I asked myself, *Am I going to make it two weeks?*

I followed up with the shrink in two weeks, feeling worse, and he changed the cocktail. This time, I believe, it was Lexapro. Same thing—come back in two weeks.

In the meantime, everything was going to hell in a handbasket. My general overall appearance, my medical practice, my marriage, and my relationship with Amanda were all falling apart.

I went back to see the shrink feeling worse. I was having suicidal thoughts. But the worst part of all of this was that I was having thoughts of harming other people. I told the shrink my fears; you would think he would be more aggressive regarding my treatment as a result. But I believe he had a plane to catch to Costa Rica for what he called a fish and fuck trip and just changed the prescription again. This time he prescribed something that was not in the class of SSRIs, Seroquel I think.

10
CHAPTER

◆

Wow, the View is Great

A s you are tired of hearing, I always wanted to provide a good life for my daughter, Amanda. So when she was born I had purchased around $8 million in term life insurance, which would last until her twentieth birthday. It was starting to seem that this investment was going to pay off in a huge way.

Way back then, the annual premium was about $6,000 a year; that was nothing. I was pulling in anywhere from $300,000 to $500,000 a year. I always lived modestly. We bought a house in Sunny Ranches, Florida, for $243,000. I drove a Chevrolet Tahoe. My wife drove anything from an SUV to a pickup truck. We weren't Mercedes people. We were simple and socking the money away.

We didn't travel. My ex had this irrational fear of flying. I had this irrational hatred of driving (it's stupid when you can fly and get there in a tenth of the time). So we never spent any money on vacations. This wasn't 100 percent Karen's fault, though it was because of her that we could only drive. The rest of the fault lay on my schedule; I worked so much we could only get away for at best three to four days.

We either went to the Florida Keys; the West Coast; or, my all-time favorite hell on earth, Satan's palace, Disney World! We must have gone to Disney thirty times, and to see the look on my wife and daughter's faces, you would think each time was their first. It got to the point I wouldn't even go to the parks. I would just chill at the hotel pool and laugh to myself looking at the tourists, knowing they had to take a second mortgage out on their house and spend their children's college funds to spend the day at the park.

That did include a soft drink. And if you didn't buy too many chocolate-covered ice cream cones and you hawked your wife's engagement ring, you could spring for a smoked turkey later in Frontier Land. I hated Disney World.

11
CHAPTER

◆

Everything is a Blur!

BACK TO LEAVING THE CONDOMINIUM BECAUSE I'D FAILED at thrusting the screwdriver into my heart. That shit hurt. I made it to the building's parking garage without being thrown in the slammer, headed up to suite 770, and was greeted by a dozen angry employees. "Gunmolly, this." "Gunmolly, that." "Call this doctor." "Bills are past due." "Gunmolly, you need to go restock this doctor's office ASAP." Yada, yada, yada, yada. I grabbed a few braces and got in the elevator. And for some reason (I do not recall), my finger pushed the button for the roof. I exited the elevator, and there was a flight of about five steps to a steel door that led to the building's roof. Surely to God, the door would be locked. The door was unlocked.

Let's go over the checklist. Bills were paid. I was going to jail anyway. I was public enemy number one in my mind, although I still hadn't committed a crime. We had plenty of savings in the banks. The house, cars, and everything I owned were paid for. I had

$8 million in life insurance. Obviously, the life insurance carriers couldn't say I'd bought the policies with this in mind, as they'd been in force for fourteen years.

Meanwhile, I was doing this while sitting on the edge of a thirteen-story building not paying attention to the police and fire department gathering below. I had checked everything off the list. Wait, I had to call my ex to say goodbye.

In the meantime, my poor partner and best friend saw my SUV was still in the garage. I could see him walking around the parking garage. I was on the phone with my wife telling her to tell Amanda—you know, the usual stuff you say when you're dangling over the edge of a thirteen-story building ready to turn what's left of your body into human burger.

I saw Jason look up, and I flipped him off. He was talking with the police officers. And I began to prepare myself for a showdown at Hallandale Beach Blvd.

Now, I was a *Forensic Files* fan. And directly adjacent to our building was another high-rise. If I were a crisis control officer, a SWAT team guy, or whoever responded to situations like this, I would do something as follows. I would take a shot from the adjacent building, trying to hit me in the shoulder to blow me back onto the roof's flat surface.

By now, I saw Jason, two police officers, and an EMT enter the building. I apologized for the language in advance and told them not to take another fucking step or I'd be doing a Peter Pan. I decided to lie down on the edge of the building for two reasons. One, I saw the news van pull up, and I didn't want to embarrass my family by being on the news without winning the lotto. But more importantly to me, I wanted to prevent the sniper in the other building from blowing my shoulder into Swiss cheese in an attempt to blow me back onto the flat surface of the building. So I pancaked down like a gray squirrel does in an oak.

Fuck you, Mr. Sniper Man.

Nothing the cops could say would sway me from my mission. It was Jason and me mano a mano for five long hours in ninety-degree heat in September on a black tar roof in South Florida. Now, I was 100 percent Italian and had beautiful bronze skin. Jason, a cornhusker from Nebraska, was as white as new-fallen snow and probably needed whole body skin grafts by the time this ordeal wrapped up five hours later. Bless his heart.

I had two problems. Jason was a huge guy—six foot three, two hundred forty pounds, all muscle—and a black belt and state of Georgia grappling champion. Jason thought I was unaware that, over the five hours, he was closing the distance from fifteen feet to now about eight feet.

The second problem—this building was designed so that about ten feet below me was a ledge. The only way for me to hit the sidewalk was to go from lying on my belly to a full standing position, in order to clear the ledge, which jetted out about eight feet from the building, and make the parking lot below. In, again, what was left of my mind, I was thinking that, if I didn't succeed in killing myself and securing my daughter's financial future, I was going to write a very strongly worded letter to the architect of this building because he'd ruined a few lives here. *How fucked up was I!?*

Back to the standoff between Jason and me. I was begging him to please let me go. "Jason, I am a prisoner in my mind," I told him. "I love you. I told my ex to give you $1 million of the life insurance money." I added that we had a $1 million Key Man policy too. I was his lottery ticket. I was the deer, and he the jaguar.

I knew how it would end. I hadn't eaten in weeks. I was down to 170 pounds from 210. Jason was in peak physical shape. He knew I was going for it, and I did.

And *damn* it; he saved my life. He lunged at me as I was going over, flipped me on my back, and threw me down on that hot as hell asphalt rock and tar roof. Jason lay on top of me, soaking wet and crying like a baby and assuring me that it was going to be OK—throwing two million bucks out the window.

All I could say to him was, "Thanks for ripping my good shirt!"

12
CHAPTER

◆

Talk about Embarrassing

So now I was handcuffed and being escorted through a parking lot full of my employees and everyone else I knew in the building. And I knew exactly where my destination was. I was going to Manor Psychiatric Hospital in Hollywood. Well, this was a very familiar address. I'd I been there hundreds of times over my twenty-two-year career fitting patients, and I was about to be one. For the first time in a long time, I was scared. No, I was terrified.

13
CHAPTER

———————— ◆ ————————

One Stop First

I WAS GOING TO DISNEY WORLD. ACTUALLY, I WOULD RATHER go to the psych hospital; it was cheaper and, quite frankly, more fun. I was in the ER first with a blood pressure of like 180/140. I remember the technician asking, "Why is your BP so high? Does it always run this high?

I specifically remember replying, "Only when I jump off a thirteen-story building without a parachute."

They gave me an IV with some wonderful cocktail in it, and I didn't care that I'd just ruined my life, my career, and the lives of my twelve employees. Whatever it was, I highly recommend it.

In walks the second love of my life—my baby sister, Alice. She always calls me babe. I love it when she does that. Apparently, her role here today was to do what every little sister should have the chance to do to their older brother who tormented their childhood—take the opportunity to have him Baker Acted.

Actually, I found out much later I was never actually Baker Acted. My sister was a brilliant lawyer, and if I understood correctly, had I been officially admitted per the Baker Act, it would have been a moniker that would have publicly stuck with my record. I only found out after discharge that I had been led to believe the Baker Act was being applied when I was technically there voluntarily and could have signed myself out AMA (against medical advice).

It was a very clever plan. Had I known this, I would have thrown myself in front of the first Greyhound bus I could find.

14
CHAPTER

◆

One Flew Over, Under, and Around the Cuckoo's nest for Twenty-Seven Days

ALK ABOUT A BUNCH OF STRANGE PEOPLE. THE STAFF WAS great. I really don't have much to say about them except the final words from my psychiatrist. I'll get back to that. As for the clientele at Hotel Weirdafornia, that's a whole different story.

First, let me remind you, I was public enemy number one in my mind. So everyone in here—and I mean everyone— was a federal agent. I could not believe the waste of our taxpayer dollars for a guy who had committed no crime.

The old guy with the sores all over his head was, hands down, the Academy Award winner. Every night before bed—and I mean every night—they covered his complete scalp and neck with this white shit that stunk and smelled like Noxzema. Guess what? He was my roommate! Why not? You would think I was a convicted serial puppy killer.

Obviously, I had very few possessions—some pajamas sent down by my ex and a picture of me and Amanda at my sister-in-law Leah's wedding. One night, it was on about day ten, I awoke to a rustling noise, only to find supercop—remember he's the Academy Award winner—in my paper bag with his hand on that picture. Big mistake. I was already going to prison for the rest of my life, and he was messing with the most important thing in the world to me—my Amanda. I beat him badly. I was like Jake LaMotta, the "Raging Bull." I had no guilt and nothing to lose—until later when I found out that he, like everyone else, was merely a patient like me suffering from one thing or the next.

What they considered punishment I enjoyed like a day at the spa. I was placed in what we patients referred to as "the rubber room."

See, I was on suicide watch, which meant, every fifteen minutes throughout the evening, an orderly would open an already half-open door and shine a flashlight in your face to make sure you were not killing yourself one way or another. What an oxymoron. We were here to supposedly get rest. Not.

So the rubber room was the Four Seasons. There were four walls, all rubber, and a mattress bolted to the floor. But most importantly, there were no flashlights. I would have loved to stay there. But no luck. So I looked for ass-whipping situations to get thrown back in. My goal while here was not to get better but to figure out how to kill myself. I scanned the place and scoped the place.

When I was in the psychiatric hospital for 31 days I was trying to find a way to kill myself. It was an impossible task. I noticed most of the breakfast, lunch and dinner trays were left with pads of unfinished butter. I was so dilusional I figured I would kill myself by eating everyone's leftover butter so as to have a massive heart attack.

They had this place figured out. There was no chance of me killing myself while an inpatient here. Then, the light bulb came on. I noticed after each meal my fellow psychos were not eating their pads of butter. That was the answer. Eat everyone's butter and die of a massive heart attack prior to discharge. How screwed up was I?

15
CHAPTER

◆

You Can't Make This Shit Up

ARRIVED AT MY HOME IN GEORGIA AT THE END OF SEPTEMBER 2007. I was completely exhausted from a month of no sleep, and my brain was functioning like a soggy marshmallow, just diluted with drugs—none of which changed my suicidal thoughts. As I previously mentioned, the only encouragement I'd received at the hospital was the life-altering advice that were my psychiatrist's final words.

> "Children of parents who commit suicide are seven times more likely to commit suicide themselves."

Three months had soon gone by, and I hadn't left the couch; I'd gone from 170 pounds to 260 pounds. All I did was cook, eat, and sleep. I was completely disengaged from my wife and child, and they from me.

I had found a psychologist and a licensed professional counselor, who, after a year's time, was successful in helping me obtain permanent disability.

On Valentine's Day 2008 my wife, on paper, only gave me the traditional meaningless candy, card, and flowers. And I gave her what she really wanted and deserved—a divorce. Prior to this move, I'd had a talk with Amanda, because I would have stayed if she'd said no. But she was with Matthew, living large, and said, "Dad, you have one life. You have to be happy." And with tears in her eyes, she gave me her blessing.

Back to Valentine's Day. Karen and I sat down, and I confirmed with Karen that she did, in fact, want a divorce. The answer I received was the only one I expected. I told her we had the most amazing child together, and no matter what, we were to remain the best of friends. And as I write this memoir, on January 27, 2021, not only have Karen and I remained the best of friends, I have also been married to Kanyon for ten years now. Karen and Kanyon are best friends and are captain and co-captain of the high school football team. Karen's fiancé and I are best friends.

Remember Kanyon from earlier? The plain young lady with the one and a half-year-old little girl called Brayly and the look of anguish on her face? Yep, she was the true love of my life. We got hitched in 2011, but it was no easy ride. We'll get there.

My divorce from Karen was final in March 2009. For the second time in my life, I felt like a complete failure—not so much as a husband but as a father. I was a good and faithful husband, and Karen was a good and maybe faithful wife. I don't know. I don't care.

But to throw a little drama in the story, when we were in court that day waiting our turn, I whispered to her, "This can't be that easy for you. For Christ's sake, we have been together for over two decades. You are the mother of our only child."

She admitted she had met someone a week earlier. I wished her well.

At the judge's podium when he declared us divorced, hand to God, in front of hundreds, we high fived. And the judge chuckled and said something to the effect of, "In all my fifty years in the legal system, I have never ..."

We walked out of the courtroom, and the first person I contacted was a man I had known for forty years, my father. The first person Karen contacted was this man she had known for one week. I will leave the rest to your imagination.

I was now on a psych disability and couldn't work, and I had become friends with a great man named Jim Sewell. Salt of the earth. Looked like he belonged on a pack of Marlboro cigarettes. A family man so tough and rugged, Jim, so I heard, once got drunk and picked a fight with a kangaroo and got his ass whipped. He owned the town's local pawn and gun shop, and we became friends.

To my surprise, I learned that his son (we'll just call him Bowser from now on because there was not a bigger ass in all of northern Georgia) was married to that sweet Southern peach Kanyon.

Well, the time came when I started volunteering in the pawn shop. Shortly after, Kanyon came to work at the shop. Now that I think about it, it was almost simultaneous. Lord, was this fate or what? I was brought up Roman Catholic and to not only believe but to practice that the vow of marriage was a sacred institution. As much as it killed me, I admired Kanyon from afar. I enjoyed her little ones, Brayly, age two, and Damian, age four, and just did my thing. I actually dated Tonya for a bit. Remember back in the beginning, she was the partner with Karen and Kanyon when the three of them formed a cheer and dance school. Hell, I might have left that part out. That was while I was still married to Karen, and I would go to the practices every now and again to admire Kanyon from afar.

We never said word one to each other. Remember she was married to Bowser and seemed content. I was smitten with Brayly, age two, and loved to play with her, even though she would break my heart by intentionally farting in my face.

As I write this memoir, she is now breaking my heart again because she suffered two cheer concussions back in November 2020, and numerous MRIs and MRAs have revealed two lesions on her brain stem that five—yes, five—Cleveland Clinic and Johns Hopkins-trained neurologists and neurosurgeons have yet to identify. At this writing, on January 28, 2021, she is now and has been suffering on average two to three gut-wrenching seizures daily that last from fifteen to twenty minutes and then, once she comes out of them, leave her paralyzed from the waist down. I don't yet know the outcome; as of this writing, we still have no answers. There has been so much tragedy in between fear that, if this ends badly, I won't be able to keep my promise to Amanda.

Back to that little firecracker who is now fighting for her life daily. I was watching her playing outside at the cheer school when she was two, and she went to run out into the street. I grabbed her arm and said, "Baby, don't run into the street. You could get hurt."

She looked at me with a look I didn't think a two-year-old was capable of making, rolled her eyes into the back of her head, and said with the cutest little Southern accent, "I ain't your baby."

Little did she know she was back then and will always be *my baby*.

So, back to be having to watch Kanyon act like she was happy being married to Bowser. He was a ladies' man, which I will never understand. He was about five foot eight at best. His face looked like a human bulldog. He had patches of hair on his lower legs like he had mange or something. I learned later that he was running around with every skank in town. And Kanyon had such low self-esteem, I truly felt she didn't think she could do any better.

I wasn't much to offer. Going through life bald, fat, and eating butter off strangers' food trays wasn't very appealing. But at least I had a huge heart, was faithful, and respected the vows a man makes to a woman. As much as it killed me, I did not stray from my beliefs, even though I heard there was strife in Kanyon's household.

16
CHAPTER

◆

The Second Best Day of My Life

ET ME TELL YOU ABOUT THE BEST DAY OF MY LIFE—OTHER than the birth of my daughter. On this particular day, we were working in the pawn shop, and I noticed my future wife looking at me like she had never looked at me before. I did so many double takes—I checked my fly; I made sure I didn't have a snot rocket hanging from my nose—I had to go see my chiropractor that afternoon.

Something had changed. It happened again. And when we had a free moment, like a leopard would pounce on its prey, I swooped my future wife up in my arms and kissed her with the passion of a Humphrey Bogart and—

Oh, sorry. I just woke up. It sounded good anyways.

I did take her by the hand, and I said, "Kanyon, I love you. I have loved you since the first time I laid eyes on you. And if you'll take a chance on me, I promise I will love, honor, and respect you for the rest of our lives."

And she took a chance on us, and every day has been honey since that day. It hasn't been easy—not because of our love for each other but because of living in a small town and some of Asshole's family—well, not some, just Asshole and his momma.

Kanyon and I were going to do it right, no matter the rumors that were flown around. We never so much as kissed until she had made him move out of her father's house. There was so much lying going on. Everyone knew Jim, God rest his soul, was doing everything in his power to get Kanyon to leave Asshole for me. He would tell her and me she deserved so much better. Everyone knew it. But Momma could not handle the truth, and neither could Asshole. Kanyon was his meal ticket. The breadwinner, the lawn mower, she did everything.

Asshole was a useless piece of shit, and I am sure he still is. I told him to prove to her that he had been faithful, and I would walk away.

He couldn't. I hired private investigators and had too much damning footage on him. He threatened me and my business.

I called him out in public, I challenging him to a modern-day public fight and inviting the town to dispel the stories behind his myth. "I have too much hatred inside for you. We're not talking about you leaving with a black eye," I told Asshole. "If you man up for once in your life, I'm going to dislocate your shoulders and both hips, give that bulldog look a free-of-charge face-lift, and put you in the hospital for a month."

As I'd expected, Asshole cowered away.

FYI, that invitation has no expiration date.

Well, I understand his Momma protecting her baby boy. All the rest of the family were and are great people. I am best friends with the oldest brother. Well, that's history.

17
CHAPTER

———————— ◆ ————————

Not Her Dream Wedding
but Mine: Yeehaw

ARE YOU FAMILIAR WITH THE IDEA THAT A WOMAN prepares for her wedding from the time she is a little girl? Well, that's how this day had to be for me. My first wedding I eloped. My second wedding was a shotgun because we were pregnant. This wedding was to be my dream wedding. This was to be my last wedding.

Neither Kanyon nor I wanted a large wedding. It was only immediate family. It was maybe twenty-five people, mostly locals from Georgia. I didn't want to inconvenience any of my out-of-town relatives. I asked them to wish us well, and we said we'd send them a few photos. We had what we all needed—each other. I don't recall there even being close friends present.

The location was a quaint bed-and-breakfast in the Blue Ridge Mountains of northern Georgia. The lake was shining, with reflection of the autumn trees. It was the end of October 2011. It was perfect.

I had known from the first moment I saw her that Kanyon was the one I had always been looking for. But when she came along down the cobblestone patch in that simple off-white dress with her two babies by her side, I was simply awestruck. I thought, *My God, what have I ever done to deserve a woman this beautiful and kindhearted?*

That answer, unfortunately, would reveal itself later in my story. Between the homemade food and the wedding cake made by Amanda, Kanyon's $100 dress, and the venue, the entire weekend had cost less than box seats at a Miami Dolphins game—maybe $4,000. It was picture postcard perfect and absolutely magical.

18
CHAPTER

◆

The Beginning of the End

GOING BACK A FEW YEARS, I HAD JUST GOTTEN DIVORCED from my ex and was living in the empty shell of our 8,000 square-foot home. It was a home that dreams were made of. It was the beginning of what would be the saddest days of my life. My oldest brother, Robert, was living in North Carolina. He was so very talented in so many genres. He had the ability to teach history at the collegiate level. He was a skilled craftsman in stained glass and succeeded at most anything he put his mind too. Ironically, we both exited failed marriages around the same time in 2010, and it really made no sense for us to live three hundred miles apart, so I convinced Robert to pack the very few possessions he had and come live with me in Jasper.

Robert, as a teenager, had been a modern-day hippy. He was an incredible artist who loved smoking weed and hashish. That was a hobby and a love he'd picked up when he was around thirteen, and he stayed strictly monogamous for the remainder of his way too short life.

For a few years, Robert worked as a waiter at the Apply Grill in Jasper and did well enough to eventually purchase a small place in Georgia. He made some decent friends outside the family circle and was doing better for himself than at any other time in his life.

One day, an ad caught my eye for a local mining company looking for a master mixologist with a chemistry background. The location and job description were right up Robert's alley. He applied for the job and landed the position. It was meant to be. Everything was going well for Robert—until he was asked to perform a task with a forklift on an unapproved ramp.

Hundreds of trips over this uneven ramp caused a collapse of numerous vertebrae in Robert's cervical spine. He took a few days off of work. I remember walking in to bring him some groceries and was mortified to find him crawling across his bedroom floor with vomitus all over his shirt and face. He couldn't find his legs.

I immediately drove him to Emory emergency room.

Knowing how workers' compensation insurance works, I knew that taking him in through the emergency room would ensure he received immediate treatment, instead of having to go through the authorization process, which could delay treatment for days. Robert was seen by Dr. Daniel Refai. To me, this young doctor might as well have been called Superman because he was out-of-this-world amazing.

Robert had sustained serious life threatening injuries as a result of the constant downward beating from the forklift jumping the unapproved ramp hundreds upon hundreds of times over the previous two-day period. We learned through MRI scans that two of Robert's cervical vertebrae had jumped facets. Not only did Robert need surgery, Robert needed life-threatening surgery. I remember Dr. Refai's exact words. "Robert has a 33 percent chance of improving, a 33 percent chance of getting worse, and a 33 percent chance of dying."

I was thinking, *I bet Robert wishes he never answered the phone when I asked him to relocate to Georgia.* I felt horrible.

The doctors placed Robert in a halo device; four bolts were screwed directly into his skull, and he was placed in forty pounds of traction for two days. The doctor's hoped to release the facets that had basically jumped their tracks.

Do you have any idea what the pressure of forty pounds of weight continuously pulling on your head and neck must feel like? It's the equivalent of being drawn and quartered—but, instead of by your limbs, by your neck.

The surgery seemed to go very well. But Robert had a very long road ahead of him, a very rocky road to say the least.

We can skip forward several months. Robert was functioning about as well as you could expect a person eating twelve oxycodone and six Soma Compound a day could. He was flat-out addicted to pain medicine, and he needed help. He needed help not now, yesterday!

19
CHAPTER

◆

Oh No! Not Momma!

T HE PHONE RANG. IT WAS MIDNIGHT. I KNEW IT WAS BAD, not because it was midnight but because the call was from my sweet sister Angel. That was her one flaw! She never called. She was the greatest wife and mother in the world, but she could easily be accused of living in her own little bubble. We'd had only one issue of difference in our past, and it was always predicated on how she kept in touch with our extended family—in that she rarely did.

Angel had an extremely busy life and career and had done very well for herself. I was proud of her accomplishments. She lived on the back burner. But when you needed her and she engaged the fight, there was no one you wanted having your back more than this feisty Italian. She was small in stature but a mountain of a woman. She got this intensity from our mother—who was, unfortunately, the reason for the late-evening call that would change my life forever in the worst and greatest of ways.

Mom had suffered a massive brain bleed and had been rushed into emergency surgery. Angel's call left me packing for a funeral.

I spent the next thirty-three days in Hollywood, Florida. I spent my mornings and afternoons fixing up her house to sell and my evenings sleeping at Mom's bedside at the rehab center so she was never alone.

Mom's recovery was amazing. Physically, she had very little deficit, and mentally she was tired. But it was clear she was never returning to her life of twenty-first-century slavery. She was coming home to Jasper, Georgia, with me—no ands, ifs, or buts.

20
CHAPTER

◆

The Brady Bunch

I N THE LATE '70S, I WAS LIVING IN SOUTH FLORIDA WITH MY mother and my two brothers and sister. We boys were seventeen, sixteen, and fifteen, and Angel was about ten. Mom never even dated much less remarried after the split from Dad. Her life was dedicated to raising her babies.

Meanwhile, back in Philadelphia, my uncle was burying his young wife, who'd just passed from breast cancer, leaving four little ones ages two, four, five, and seven. Tony, my uncle, was a cop. He was a great man, but he was the most absolutely useless human being on planet earth. He couldn't even put together a ham and cheese sandwich on his own.

Mom called the audible. "Kids, our family up north needs help, and we're moving back to Philadelphia to become the Brady bunch."

And so we were—Mom, useless Tony, six boys, and two girls.

I was thinking, *This is great. I get to forgo my senior year in high school in sunny South Florida.* I'd been attending John Bartram High School, where my little brother David and I were the only two white guys. Awesome.

"Hey, Dave. How many times did you get your ass kicked today? Only three. So you had a good day."

I believe this was where my heart began to harden.

21
CHAPTER

♦

My Brother David:
The Best Man I Know

DAVID WAS THE ONLY MEMBER IN OUR FAMILY WHO I FELT had it figured out from day one. He was not the most educated. As a matter of fact, I believe he had a GED. But he did very well for himself. He worked for everything he had. He never lived his life based on what was convenient for him. And family was always his number one priority.

When I was attending my butter-eating seminar in 2007, David drove down from North Carolina to sit by my side every day. I vividly remember David holding my hand, telling me it was going to be OK.

I found out months later that David had gone through a bout of depression as a result of my experience, and this broke my heart.

Once again, as I write these very words on January 28, 2021, I have spiraled from the stress over Brayly's condition, and David has shown up for me. He came last night to make sure I was OK.

He is my *hero*. If there is one favor I hope God grants to me it's to please take me first. I could not bear the loss of my David!

22
CHAPTER

———————◆———————

Day of Discharge

OR THIRTY DAYS, I SPENT MY ENTIRE WAKING HOURS painting, replacing carpet, and fixing odds and ends at Mom's home while her infinitely useless husband, Tony, sat on the patio staring into oblivion, devastated that his twenty-first-century slave was no longer at his beck and call.

Don't get me wrong. Tony was a good man and husband in most ways; he was just 100 percent dependent on Mom. He was a cop from Philadelphia who earned a salary of $18,000 a year when he was hurt on a burglary call and was forced into retirement. I was amazed at the $600,000 nest egg they had accumulated into retirement. Years back, they had made me executor of his estate. It was these funds that afforded me the ability to hire a private nurse for Mom when I brought her back to my place in Jasper, Georgia.

Mom and I were set to leave upon her discharge, and Tony and my stepbrother, little David, were to follow in his car with the two family dogs. During Mom's stay in rehab almost twenty-seven days, Tony had become very dark, and he'd never visited Mom in rehab—not one time. His drinking, which had always been extreme, had destroyed his liver, and it now greatly worsened. He became severely depressed. As our departure date to Jasper approached, Tony started to come up with excuses, saying that, instead of caravanning with us, he would follow later. I knew he had no intention of ever making the trip. Little did he know, I had already removed his service revolver from his end table.

The little respect I had for the man was gone. Mom had given up her life to raise his children and had, in essence, been a twenty-first-century slave to this man for thirty plus years. But now that she served no purpose, she meant nothing to him.

One month later, little David and Tony would arrive in Jasper. Tony would look like he'd put himself through further hell—and he had. He wouldn't be in Jasper for two weeks before he'd be rushed to the hospital in total organ failure. He would pass a week later.

Meanwhile, I bought a minivan, and Mom and I were heading home to Jasper. Kanyon had made all the arrangements I'd asked of her while I was in Florida. She had ordered an adjustable orthopedic bed. We had a walk-in tub/shower installed. Kanyon took the wheel in Georgia.

I had asked Robert to find Mom a neurologist and an internist. His feedback was far from impressive. I knew exactly what was going on.

23
CHAPTER

◆

An Absolute Privilege

MOM WAS ADJUSTING WELL. KANYON AND THE KIDS HAD been great. They accepted Mom as their own, and I couldn't be more pleased with how things were going. The ability to care for the one who has cared for you is an absolute privilege. My mother had spent her entire life as a servant to her family. She had never seen the world, eaten at fine restaurants, or been to the theater until now. It was my intention to spoil my mother, and we did.

Mom recovered from her stroke physically very well, but her memory was greatly affected. This was a blessing in disguise. Months and months had passed, and Mom never mentioned Tony. I just assumed the good Lord had done her a solid and erased that part of her memory; either that or the memory loss was a result of the anesthesia from Mom's brain surgery.

The surgeon did a biopsy on Mom's brain and informed us that Mom had an amyloid protein in her body. The best way it was explained to David and me was that the blood vessels in Mom's brain were the equivalent of an old garden hose that could burst at any time. Mom could live a month or ten years following the surgery. Mom was a walking time bomb.

I had placed Robert's needs on the back burner because mom was my number one priority at the moment. That was the biggest mistake of my life. I only had time to devote to the care of one of them, and I chose my mom. I was stretched thin. This audible brought me close to breaking a promise I had made to myself when I left the psychiatric facility so many years back. To save one's life, I had to forgo the life of another. That was a burden no one should ever have to bear.

24
CHAPTER

$\blacklozenge$

A Heartbreak

WE FOUND ROBERT'S BODY IN THE WOODS BEHIND MY house. Nothing you can ever do in your lifetime can prepare you for finding a body in the woods, much less the body of someone who has frozen to death, much less the body of your best friend, much less the body of your brother. Robert was exactly one year and ten days older than me and two years older than David. We were like the Three Musketeers and had the greatest childhood ever. We were poor as shit, but we had each other.

I was the brother that was into sports, David was into fixing things and cars, and Bob was into weed and selling weed. There is not a whole lot to say except even though we were three different personalities, we were three amigos and were always there for each other.

After high school we went in different directions. Robert never really made much of himself. He had two failed marriages, never had a relationship with his two sons, and did a felony rap in Florida for theft. The love of his life was weed.

25
CHAPTER

───────◆───────

Robert's Decline

Back when Mom was in rehab in Florida, everyone was pulling his or her own weight to prepare for Mom's arrival in Jasper—everyone except Robert. The simplest of tasks were being meet with the greatest of excuses. Something was up, and I knew exactly what it was. The doctors had slowly cut Robert off of the pain medicines that had caused his addictions. And for the first time in his life, he decided to reach out for something to replace that feeling. That something was meth!

I can't say as I blame him. Robert was an adventurer. He loved to camp, hike, boat, fish, and kayak. His spinal injury took that all away from him. He could walk, but it was very uncoordinated. He certainly couldn't work. The love of his life had always been weed, but that brought a mellowing effect. He needed a high that gave him energy. And for the first time in his life, he was going to be unfaithful. I got so tired of the lies I just started looking the other way.

He could not stop scratching his eyes. It had gotten so bad that he tore the retina in his right eye. And after numerous visits and surgeries, he lost the sight in the eye, and it clouded over. He also wasn't into personal hygiene, and the top four front teeth in his mouth were missing. He was no looker.

Robert's meth abuse had gotten so bad he was suffering from tremendous paranoia. He was living in one of my rentals and absolutely destroyed the place, with four dogs crapping and urinating all over the place. He barricaded each and every window and door.

His mania was so bad that he'd called me one day to tell me he had killed an intruder. Robert was a felon and asked that I tell the police that I had done the killing, and the gun was mine. I said, "Yeah, I will get right on that."

Kanyon and I drove right over. There was no intruder. He had shot a few holes in the living room floor.

I asked Kanyon to call the police, knowing the only way he was getting better was if he did some major time and detoxed. The police were called. I cannot tell you how much I enjoyed pouncing on him and punching the shit out of his ribcage while we awaited the police arrival. He was arrested. He was a felon. They found guns, ammo, marijuana, and meth. *This is good*, I thought. *He will thank me later.*

I didn't care if he would. He would out of my life for years, and I could focus on our mother.

I got the call from Robert the next day. "Bring me my wallet. I have bailed out."

What?!

Before I brought the wallet, I asked to visit the judge. I asked the judge to reconsider, stating that Robert was out of his bloody mind and that he would kill me, himself, or some innocent party. The judge stated that everyone was entitled to bail. I looked the judge in the face, called him a fucking asshole, and said, "You can't be this stupid!

Four years later, that very judge was arrested for over fifty counts of financial theft from the office of the magistrate. Don't drop the soap!

Just recently and four years after Robert's death, it was reelection time in our small town of thirty thousand people. The political mudslinging was at an all-time high, and the dirt of politics in this good-old-boy town was revealed—in a big way. Corruption at all levels was revealed.

Criminals who should have never been released, such as Robert, only cost money being housed in jail. Put those criminals back on the street and make them attend drug court twice a week at a fee, and the piggy bank, which never really is accounted for, gets full—quite full.

Well, Robert bonded out that very day. And gratefully, he was sentenced to drug court, which in essence meant he had to be drug tested twice weekly. That would keep him on the straight and narrow.

Fast-forward a year later. I went to pick Robert up to take him to an eye appointment; he was legally blind from clawing out his eye. He had relied on me to drive him for a year, and he was nowhere in sight. His car was there, so I figured maybe someone had taken him to his drug court appointment, and I would make use of this time to clean up his shithole.

No sign of Robert, so I drove down to the drug court office to enquire if he had been there this morning, only to find out that he hadn't been there in over a year. I asked, "Well doesn't that mean a warrant should have been placed for his arrest?"

"Yes," she replied, "a bench warrant."

Then I got the news.

For the very first time in my life, I didn't know what to do. I wanted very much to go to my wife. I needed her to hold me and tell me it was going to be OK.

Detective Mustgrave made me sit down for a minute to collect myself. It seemed like hours. I wanted Kanyon. After what seemed like an eternity, I walked to the car, opened the door, collapsed into her arms, and screamed uncontrollably. "They found him! Bob's dead. Bob froze to death. Oh my God, Kanyon! Oh my God!"

After I composed myself, I called my father and broke the news.

And I swear to God, the words out of his mouth were, "I can't believe this is happening the day before I leave for California!"

I asked him to contact Angel and Alisa. I just could not break the news to my sweet sisters. I told him I would call David.

26
CHAPTER

◆

Inconveniences

I FEEL HORRIBLE ABOUT SPEAKING ILL OF THE DEAD, BUT I just believe there are things in life people should not get away with. My father was all about convenience in life. He was brilliant, as I previously mentioned. He was embarrassingly frugal. I wouldn't go out to eat with him unless I paid, because he would find a way to complain about the bill to get out of it. He had a coupon for everything.

He had many great lifelong friends, and one thing I never understood was why, in life, he treated his friends better than he did his family but not in death. When his closest friends or even family had past, if it was inconvenient, which was 99 percent of the time, he skipped the funeral. This I will never understand. I always thought he was going to be the loneliest man in the funeral home.

My stepmom, Christine, would have no such thing. Mom honored Dad in three beautiful ceremonies across three states. The first was in Ventura, California, with about 50 people. The second was in Ft. Lauderdale, Florida, with about 100 people. Lastly, she held a ceremony in Banner Elk, North Carolina, with about 150 people.

He was a lackluster father and husband and in no way deserved this honor. It is a testament to the kind of wife and woman Christine is. She is the star here. And I for one am a better person for having Momma Chris in my life. I adore you, Mom.

27
CHAPTER

◆

The Sacrificial Anode

DAD HAD BECOME SUCH A BURDEN ON MOMMA CHRISTY. I hated the way he treated me during my life. I could not even imagine living with the man full-time. I found him very intimidating during the day, but he drank his sorrows away, and he drank heavily. The man knew no moderation; nor did he acknowledge the burden he placed on Mom. There was the constant verbal abuse and the physical abuse he placed on himself from his drunken falls. I never witnessed any physical abuse against Momma, but I am not naive enough to believe it wasn't there. I did lose what very little bit of respect I had left for him when he threw the TV remote control and hit Mom in the head with it.

As much as I didn't want to, I witnessed his downward spiral and knew what I had to do. I started converting my lower two-car garage into an apartment for Dad. There had been a few innuendos from Mom in the past. They were very subtle pleas, usually when

Mom was at her wit's end during another ER visit while in Ventura, California.

I always said Ventura was not good for Dad. It seemed like he would spend most of his time there in and out of the hospital regardless. I could handle him better than anyone. I was retired, bored and always considered myself a sacrificial anode. For those who don't know, a sacrificial anode is an aluminum plate on a boat's motor that makes the saltwater attach itself to the anode so as to protect the rest of the motor. I was the human form for my family.

There was no plan in place, but I could see Dad was becoming a burden to Mom, and I wanted to do my part. So, I started to convert one of my two-car garages into an apartment for Dad. It would be great. We could play poker with the guys, and he could do his all-time favorite pastime—browse for coupons and spend his entire day putting together lunches. We would attend those lunches; he would eat nothing and pass his lunch out to everyone else at the table. This was what his amazing career had culminated into. I don't know why, but I found this existence not only annoying but also absolutely pathetic.

I was about an hour into the apartment project when I received the call that Dad was back in the emergency room. But this time it was comical. As you know, marijuana was legal in California. Mom or my sister Alisa had asked one of her friends for some THC-laced candies to help control my dad's chronic back pain, but Dad knew nothing of this. One afternoon, Dad, who, like me, has a sweet tooth saw the candies on the counter and ate all three. I did the math; it was the equivalent of a first-time pot smoker ingesting about two joints.

Dad and Mom were attending my nieces Hailey and Noelle's production of one thing or another. The girls, like their mother and grandmother, were both lovers of the arts and both very talented and beautiful ballerinas. Dad started losing feeling in his lower legs and told Mom to call an ambulance in the middle of the production. One way or another, the man brings chaos with him wherever he goes.

At the ER, he was poked and prodded, and the look on his face when they told him he was stoned had to be priceless. Alisa sent me the cutest video of the man eating hospital pasta, stating it was the finest he had ever had. This was a man who rented a chalet in the South of Italy with a private chef for a month, devouring the best pasta he had ever eaten in his life lying in a hospital bed in Ventura, California. Dad's next visit would not be that far off and not so comical.

28
CHAPTER

◆

Headache

KANYON WAS TEACHING A CLASS ONE DAY, AND SHE experienced an intense piercing pain right on the top of her skull. It was so intense it brought her to her knees, and she vomited. My wife the trooper shook it off and, later that evening, explained what had occurred. I made an appointment for Kanyon to see our local neurologist, and he ordered an MRI of her brain.

Meanwhile, back in California, Dad had an episode. Dad was found by Mom on the floor. He had fallen through a coffee table, and there was glass everywhere. Mom, to the best of her ability, couldn't get his beaten body off the floor. So the ambulance was called. Dad's vitals were all over the place. Normally, Dad would come in for a tune-up and the resilient SOB would get a tune-up and an oil change and be sent on his way. But this time was different.

I caught the next flight to LAX. You've heard the old saying that doctors make the worst patients? Well, it could not have been truer. I stayed on the couch in Dad's hospital bed twenty-four seven for five straight days, only to hear him second-guess every decision his doctors made for him and question every medication they prescribed for him. It was hell. He was hell.

In the meantime, I got the call from my wife saying that the results from her MRI were in. The news was devastating. She had a Chiari malformation of the brain. In essence, her brain was too large for her skull, which was causing pressure, leading to the intense headaches. She needed brain surgery. She was inconsolable.

Here I was, thousands of miles away from the most important person in the world to me, who needed me right now, sitting with a man who, when I needed him the most, never once came to me in my need and who was doing everything in his power to not listen to his doctors. I told my dad my wife needed me and that I had to go to her. He asked me how I knew she truly had a Chiari malformation. I called his hand. I showed him the MRI.

His exact words were, "Kanyon does not have a Chiari malformation."

I had bluffed. The MRI I'd showed him was an MRI from a Johns Hopkins' study of a Chiari malformation patient. I called him an asshole. He called me a double asshole. And I left, hoping to never see him again. For the first time in my life, I felt vindicated!

I took Kanyon to see an Emory-trained neurosurgeon. The surgical options were explained. We sought the help of a migraine specialist, and through a procedure called dry needling and medications, Kanyon's migraines have almost completely subsided.

On the West Coast, poor Mom and Alisa had had a horrific time with Dad ping-ponging between the emergency room and back. This time, Dad's hospital stay might be permanent. I needed to get back out there, as I felt extremely uneasy about our last exchange and hadn't spoken with him since.

This time, David joined me in Ventura California. Dad looked very frail. The look on his face when I walked into the room was priceless. It was the look of sheer appreciation and joy! I sat with him, and we joked a bit about bananas of all things. They were trying to get his potassium levels up, and they were giving him this awful-tasting liquid to raise his levels. He told me they wouldn't give him real bananas because they were too expensive. I told him I doubted that was the reason and, only to prove him fallible, I asked the doctor, who explained he would have had to eat over twenty bananas to equal that awful liquid. I felt great.

Anyway, they catheterized Dad, and what very little came out looked like iced tea. It was clear he was in kidney failure. That was the beginning of his end. That evening when I left, for the first and last time in my life, my father told me he loved me back. I knew then I would never hear those words come from him again. What was worse, he knew it too.

29
CHAPTER

◆

How Do I Justify Divine Intervention?

I AM FAR FROM A LITERARY PERSON. AS A MATTER OF FACT, IF it wasn't required reading in school or published in *Car and Driver,* I assure you I have not read it. I am type A to the core and way too hyper to get into reading a good book when I can be unclogging a toilet or mowing my lawn.

How do I justify divine intervention? I have the least creative mind in the history of pen and paper. But within the past week— yes, just the past week—I and everyone I know has noticed a change in my mood and behavior. And it is in no way positive. I can't help but think it has to do with the recent unjustified diagnosis given to my daughter by one of the most respectable hospitals in the Atlanta area—this diagnosis that might as well be a bullet to the brain.

30
CHAPTER

◆

This All Began November 2, 2020

HAD BEEN OVERWHELMED WITH GRIEF—NOT SO MUCH grief for myself but grief for my sweet wife Kanyon. I'd been obsessed with finding a cure for my daughter, which no doctor had been able to do. You might think, *What kind of father would not be grieving over the diagnosis of bilateral brain lesions of the basil ganglia in his fun-loving, brilliant, carefree seventeen-year-old daughter?* Well, let me explain why I'd become numb and just downright hardened to heartache. It was a curse that had plagued the core of my existence, beginning with the tragic death of my best friend and older brother Robert.

"Hey, Bob. I'm getting divorced. Why don't you come live with me down here in Jasper?"

My wife had always been there for me, helping me get through the gut-wrenching, take-your-own-life pain that I'd suffered consistently from December 2015 until November 2020. I would challenge the mightiest demon to prevent my sweet Kanyon from experiencing one-one thousandth of that kind of heartache. She is too good and too pure to ever have to feel this. This angel saved my life, and I can't fail her. I won't fail her.

I've placed so much unnecessary pressure upon myself this past week that something has happened in my very soul. My diseased brain is using my hands as a vehicle to produce these words. I would love to take credit for this. But this is truly divine intervention. I have to prevail—not for me, not for Brayly, but for sweet Kanyon. Kanyon's love for me has never faltered. She has the strength of ten Hercules. I owe her everything.

Something has opened a door in my brain that I hope closes soon. While it's exciting to have a purpose, this power scares the hell out of me. This person scares the hell out of me and everyone around me. I told Kanyon I wanted out of this marriage last night. This is not me. I never wanted to be a writer. I will never write again. I do not know whether it's divine or not, but for some reason, for someone's benefit—certainly not mine—this story must be told.

Everyone wants last week's Gunmolly back. So do I. I have the energy of a fifteen-year-old. I am constantly jacked up. I kid you not. I have slept an average of two hours per day for the past three weeks. I don't do drugs, but you would think I inhale an eight ball of cocaine a day.

31
CHAPTER

◆

Fate

I'D MET PEOPLE IN THE LAST TWO MONTHS AFFILIATED WITH the Amen Clinic. I had no business meeting. I believe it was all to guide us to them—not only for the sake of my daughter Brayly and her seizure disorder but also to see what the hell is going on in my brain.

As exciting as it may be, I was quite scared to learn what was going on. My life since 2015 had been ravaged by tragedy. It was just par for the course. I guess it was my turn.

As if crying every night because you were failing the absolute *love* of the most deserving woman God has put on this earth wasn't enough, wait, now I was failing her regarding finding out what was wrong with our daughter and now me. I'd lost fifty-two pounds in the last three months.

Dear *God*, please take me because I am in no way afraid to meet you. I look forward to bowing at your feet. I pray to you every night and thank you for the blessings that you've bestowed upon me and my family. My faith has never wavered and never will. I've been put through hell and back. But for the love of all that is holy, please don't cause me to make this woman shed a tear on my account. This I could not bear.

It was November 2, 2020, a normal winter day for Bre. She stopped at Chickfil-A to get her normal carb overload on the way to practice at Tag Gymnastics—a number one with a fruit slushie and fries. Chickfil-A had the drive-through down to a science, and she knew she wouldn't be late to practice. It was a normal afternoon snack in the life of a teenager prior to practice.

At practice, she called, "Hey, Mom! Watch *me*! I'm going to try and land my back tuck."

"Oh my God. Are you OK?"

Bre had landed on her left shoulder and forehead. But she shook it off like a trooper and continued with practice. She came home with a headache but nothing too serious—or so we thought.

Fast-forward a couple of days. Dad was in the kitchen cooking spaghetti. Bre and Mom walked in about 6:30 p.m. Bre was crying and holding a bag of ice against her upper lip and mouth. Her eyes were swollen, and she'd clearly been crying. She had just returned home from evening cheer practice. During practice, she was basing a flyer. The girl who was flying was a tiny little thing, weighing no more than eighty-five pounds. This time, she'd come down wrong and elbowed Bre smack in the mouth. The flyer might as well have been a sack of bowling balls as hard as she hit Bre in the face. Bre was convinced her upper teeth were loose, and she had one hell of a headache. This was November 4, 2020.

Bre went to school as usual, though she had a stiff neck and a slight headache. She gave it a two on a scale of ten.

Friday Evening, the night before the competition's team first competition, a couple of the girls met to get spray tanned for the competition. Bre had been spray tanned before. But this time would be the beginning of the last day of what she used to call a normal life.

Bre walked into the spray booth, and once the spray tanning began, she immediately began losing her hearing in her left ear. Next, she vomited and completely blacked out for twenty plus minutes.

The next thing she remembered was waking up in the ambulance heading to the ER in Canton, Georgia.

The following Monday, I took Bre to a concussion specialist, who told us the effects of a concussion and explained that they could last for weeks to as long as several months and provide us with concussion protocols. We were to return in two weeks.

A few days later, Bre started to black out every two to three days, and the blackouts lasted for what seemed forever. The scary part was that, when she recovered, she couldn't get her legs back for nearly an hour.

I decided to take Bre to see my buddy Jon Wis DC. Jon was a very fine chiropractor who treated all the local school athletes. He was a man of great faith and had a lovely wife and five daughters. That alone, tells you he is a man with patience. Anyhow, I asked Jon to shed some light on the situation—to take a few X-rays and between his knowledge and my thirty years in orthopedics, maybe we could find something the ER had missed.

Jon's Xrays revealed moderate scoliosis and a jaw that looked like it had gone a few rounds with Mike Tyson. Jon stated, "Her dang jaw is dislocated." This could very well be causing the loss of hearing she experienced before she blacked out, as well as the blackouts themselves.

Jon also said, "Gunmolly, sports concussions can and do open the door in the brain to seizures. You should look into that as well."

Then out of nowhere Bre started seizing right on the table. I asked Jon what I should do and moved through the process. The hospital rooms were nicer than most hotel rooms I'd stayed in, and they offered room service. This place had it going on. I mentioned the possibility of the jaw dislocation to the hospitalist. He touched her cheeks and immediately dispelled this diagnosis. I jumped hi s ass and told him, "*Do not* discredit this idea without further investigation."

The care team did the routine blood work and urine samples and started an IV.

Members of the pediatric neurology team arrived, assessed B, and ordered a video EEG of the brain. About four hours later, B looked like a human Q-tip.

In the meantime, she was sedated with Tramadol and some other things. For two or three days, the only thing the hospital captured was a blackout that lasted l about three seconds in duration. My wife and I had noticed that, during the two days of monitoring, a good 30 percent of the time, the monitors weren't even attached.

The day of discharge arrived. The neurology team presented with the coolest psychiatrist *ever*. He was a handsome middle-aged man dressed like a yoga instructor—a guy who, in your mind, you could just tell was into herbs, chanting. and all that stuff. We dug him. He took Bre off her Prozac and changed it to Lexapro because another member of our family had used it successfully, and studies show a correlation of synergistic benefits between drug interaction and family members.

The doctor told B to get into yoga, take her meds, do exercises with no impact to the brain, and go on with her life. Sounded great.

"Wait a minute, Doc. What's causing the blackouts and seizures?" Here it comes.

"The MRI shows a spot on the brain in the basil ganglia area. We cannot identify what it is. Could be a lesion, glioma, infection, contusion, demyelination of cells. But it's in an area of the brain that's difficult to biopsy. So we're just going to watch it and revisit with another MRI in four months."

Oh my God, OK. "So her diagnosis is?"

"Bre has what is called PNES (psychogenic nonepileptic seizures). These are seizures that occur as a result of psychological causes such as severe mental illness. Bye now! Have a great day!"

The misses and I looked at each other. *Severe mental illness?*

I left the situation impressed with the square footage of the rooms and the room service but nothing else. And we sought several other opinion s.

In the meantime, I exhaustively researcher PHENS to find there is no treatment from a pharmacological standpoint.

The only treatment is cognitive behavior therapy.

Do you ever have déjà vu?

The universe is filled with wonder. About four months back, my son Damian, out of the blue, started having severe panic attacks—like every day. The kid was beside himself freaking out in the middle of the night. He lost his job, stopped hanging with his friends, and split with his girlfriend. He was pathetic.

Finding a decent shrink in and around this area has always been a chore. Remember, I like to sit on the edge of thirteen-story buildings and eat stranger's dollops of butter on occasion. So I knew.

I took Damian to our local ER so many times the running joke when we walked in the door was, "Good morning or afternoon or evening"—it was that many times—"Damian and Mr. Kodiad. Are we having another heart attack today?

I had finally had it with Damian, and I said, "Son, you *do not* have a heart attack twenty-four seven for three months straight. If you're having a damn heart attack, please get it over with because they're having a sale on coffins at Fred's General down the road a ways."

He drove us crazy, but after our doctor tried several cocktails Lexapro seemed to work. This was what I meant about pharmacology and genetics. It had worked for Damian, so they thought it may work for Bre. Good in theory.

32
CHAPTER

◆

Stressed to the Max

HAVE ONE GUILTY PLEASURE. I HAVE TWO BLOWN SHOULDERS, both of which have had major rotator cuff surgery. I can't golf because of my shoulders. And remember, I am type A as hell. So if we can't play bumper golf carts on an outing, I will pass. Hell, if I can't sleep at night, I turn on a baseball game. That's the best tranquilizer for me.

Let's get to my guilty pleasure. I love to get a massage every two weeks. I'd been going to our local massage therapist, Mary, for years, and we'd become great friends. Hell, she'd seen me naked more times than my wife. Now to think of it, that might explain why I saw her laughing every time we ran into each other at the local high school football game.

On this particular day, Mary was training a new therapist and asked if I didn't mind having a session with her and to give her some feedback. I happily obliged. Sue was the therapist's name. And until my session, I had never met someone who loved to talk as much as I do. The massage was fantastic, but the conversation was even better.

Sue's full-time job was counseling patients (mostly youth and troubled teen)s for addictions and what not and teaching them how to cope with anxiety; depression; and then she said it, *panic attacks.* I damn near rolled off the table. This was fate. *You couldn't make this shit up.*

Well the Lexapro had kicked in for Damian, and we didn't utilize Sue for him. But I called her immediately for Bre. Sue started coming to our home every Sunday morning. The sessions seemed to make Bre feel positive, and Bre had connected with Sue. But then the seizures came right back.

Sue suggested I look into the Alon Clinic in Atlanta for a complete workup of Bre's brain. The clinic offered SPECT imaging, which is a 3D scan and then the results were analyzed by psychologists, not physicians. Based on their findings, patients were treated holistically, pharmaceutically, and naturally in an effort to make sure their brains were working at full capacity. It was all about blood flow in the brain. This was very impressive work going on at the Alon Clinic. We are up to about one seizure every other day now. It was the end of December.

Bre had a complete cardiac workup with Skipe Heart, including wearing a heart monitor for five days. We pushed a button each and every time Bre seized. She got a clean bill of health on her heart.

We had a second opinion with a well-known pediatric neurologist, who was kind enough to see us at 6:00 p.m. as a new patient. Who does that? We brought the discs of the previous MRI with us, but unfortunately the computers were down.

As I explained the previous weeks' events, the look on the new doctor's face became quite alarming. The doctor stated, "I'm sending you to the ER right now, and I'm ordering two new MRIs and two new MRAs—two of the brain and two of the cervical spine."

I asked the doctor her concerns.

She said, "I know exactly what is wrong with Bre."

My wife and I, while relieved to have an answer, were mortified about the words that soon would exit her mouth. We had to rule out a blockage, a tear in an artery, a stroke, or something that was preventing blood from getting to the brain. Two things could cause vassal vagal episodes (blackouts)—lack of sufficient blood to the brain and/or the out. Remember, the heart was cleared.

So, I Mario Andrettied it to the nearest ER. The doctor had called, and the ER staff was expecting us. Radiology reports and a follow-up phone call showed the same spots seen on previous imaging, and these two practitioners also told us they had no idea what it was. Exit stage left.

The next doctor, another pediatric neurologist who found not one spot but two, said for the third time, "I have no idea what these spots are."

I finally, in frustration, said, "Do they not teach a course in medical school on alien tracking device implantation?"

At this point, I'd had it with neurologists, and I was searching for the most well-trained pediatric neurosurgeon who specialized in the removal of superterrestrial implantation tracking devices model R2sl. And I couldn't find him.

The next doctor was a cool guy. He was cool because he was nerdy as hell but he tried to engage with the teenagers with his verbiage and in the way he carried himself. When Bre would answer his questions, he would always follow with, "Very cool."

Unfortunately, for the fourth time, he saw the spots, stated he'd as seen similar spots in other patients in the past, and added he had no idea what they were.

What?!

He stated the spots were in a much too dangerous area to work with and that he might do more damage trying to biopsy them. His suggestions were like the previous suggestions. Leave them alone and revisit with a repeat MRI in four months to see if they have changed or if Darth Vader had taken them back while Bre was asleep one night.

The seizures were now happening daily with greater intensity. They lasted about three to six minutes but then the recovery was a good thirty minutes plus before she had enough strength to get her legs.

At this point, I was starting to develop the John Q mentality. Anyone who has seen the film can relate to what I'm talking about. I couldn't do that. Too many people depended on me, and I didn't want to become the bride of Dirk's on cell block 8.

Kanyon was my last marriage. Sorry, at this point, something is starting to change in my personality. I'm becoming much angrier. Everyone sees it except me. I'm just so angry at the outrageousness of this situation. I can't eat. I'm down another ten. I'm averaging maybe one to two hours of sleep per night. Yet, I have so damn much energy and feel so alive. I can't sit still, so I start writing about my life. These are my word, every last one of them, but I *do not* know where they're coming from. My hands are simply the vehicle hitting the keyboard. But the inspiration to get this story out is coming from another power.

It's exciting because, since I've been retired, I feel like I have no purpose. I've been wanting to go back to work for so long, but something always gets in the way—taking care of others, whether it be my brother, my mother, or someone else. Don't get me wrong. Taking care of your mother is an absolute privilege—one every child should be humbled to experience.

I just landed a job delivering fresh produce locally part-time. Remember, I have the medical knowledge to earn $500,000 a year and did for decades, but I wanted a job with no stress.

Remember how well the butter eater deals with stress. I would deliver horseshit if it was stress free. The doctors say Bre can't drive, work, or attend school. She's on hospital homebound and can't be left alone. Guess what my new career is? Full-time babysitter.

I have the resources to remain retired, but let's talk about my father and stepmother Christy for a bit. The topic oh so relevant when it comes to the man I grew up to be.

My relationship with my father was strange and really didn't develop until I graduated from FSU and moved to Hollywood, Florida, in 1985. I was working in my father's office as his cast technician and learned what I know today. Hence, I'm very well educated in orthopedics and a great researcher of useless knowledge.

And when it came to raising my children, I didn't want to be anything like him. My birth parents divorced when I was around six. Dad was a resident at a children's hospital in Miami, Florida. He worked his ass off and made a name for himself to provide for his family. But my birth mother, who was an Italian from Philadelphia and quite frankly only high school educated, just didn't like the fact that he was never around. It was no one's fault. They just had different ideas on marriage and their career aspirations.

Anyway, they divorced. And sometime later, Dad met a pediatric nurse named Christy Ericks. I could understand the attraction. Tall, beautiful, and blond with blue eyes of Nordic descent, Christy was career motivated as well. It was a good match. Little did I know, many years later, they would give me one of the greatest joys in my life—my little sister Alice.

I had to have my tonsils and adenoids removed. I guess I was about seven or eight. And little did I know, this lovely nurse was going to be my momma one day. That's what we call them here in Jasper. Anyway, she cared for me after my surgery, and all I remember was an unending supply of some kind of gum and ice cream ordered by my future momma. She won my heart back then and has kept it to this day. She has a heart of gold, love the arts, and giving to charitable associations like the Ronald McDonald House, St. Jude Hospital, cancer associations, and handfuls of others. She has provided well for her children and grandchildren. I hope she outlives me. I could not bear to lose Momma.

Anyhow, momma had me at bubblegum and ice cream. Dad was altogether different—well with me anyway. Shortly after the divorce, his visitation went from every weekend to once a month, and soon I would see him less and less often. It was in no way his fault; he was building an orthopedic empire. That meant absolutely nothing to me until I really got to know the man after I started working for him when I was twenty-three years old.

Prior to that, he intimidated the hell out of me. When in college I wrote to him, he actually took the time to write back—well kind of. He took the letter; correct my grammatical errors in red ink; and sent the letter back with a sticky note attached, stating, "This is what I'm paying for?"

I didn't blame him. That letter had a lot of red ink on it. I wrote my father one letter in my lifetime.

My dad and Momma Christy have a second home in the mountains of North Carolina, where they would spend the summers. I mentioned this because I had a knack for ruining many of their summer vacations. Remember the mental hospital thing where I became a butter connoisseur? That occurred during the summer. He never came to visit me in the twenty-seven days I was there. But he made it quite clear he micromanaged the stay from his home in North Carolina. There were two other occasions where I almost died from massive GI bleeds—the first one requiring fifteen units of blood transfusions. Five years later, it happened again, requiring ten units of blood transfusions. Anyhow, it was summertime; he was on vacation. And he never came home to visit but made it clear he micromanaged everything by phone.

I don't blame him. As a child, he was raised by two very strict, poor Italian immigrants who were incapable of showing affection. Unfortunately, some of that trait was passed onto him. I have told my dad I love him a thousand times in my lifetime, and he could only say it back about three times. But that was in his final years, and it seemed he had to force himself to do it.

I know he loved us because he worked hard, built a legacy, and provided for his children and grandchildren. He sacrificed his relationships with us so as to be able to provide for us and future generations down the road. Had he not been able to do so, it would have all been for nothing.

As I mentioned earlier, the one thing I took the most from my father and my relationship with him is that you never put anything above your children. If Kanyon or the kids needed me, and I was far away, I would crawl through hell and back to get to them. This fear of not being able to get to my loved ones in need took a great toll on my mental health w h e n the girls moved from Florida to Georgia. I learned from my experience. Separation *does not* work.

I was bored. I'd been retired for fifteen years a t this point and had plenty of free time. Just kidding. I couldn't stand to see the anguished look on my wife's face any longer; it broke my heart, and it became my quest and my mission to fix Bre. I had to start thinking outside the box. I started thinking of everything from environmental factors to allergies.

I was hoping it was my wife's cat—$1,500, smashed-faced, exotic male Persian shit ass demon spawn from hell who ruined a couch every four months because my wife didn't have the heart to let me have it declawed as a kitten. So now we had an annual budget of $5,000 for living room furniture. We shopped at the thrift store! That got us about a couch every twelve weeks.

Dad, what would you like for your birthday?

A couch.

Same question and answer on Father's Day and Christmas.

33
CHAPTER

◆

Alzheimer's

I NEVER WANTED TO LIE TO MY MOTHER, BUT THERE WERE two great tragedies in her life that she did not need to know about—and for the first time, her disease was beneficial to her—the deaths of her husband and her firstborn son, Robert.

Alzheimer's is devastating not only to those who suffer from it but also to those who watch their loved ones decay because of it. Mom had begun showing signs of the disease in her late sixties, but they were just written off as senior moments. The surgery after the stroke and brain bleed really impacted her memory, which was *great*! After Mom's thirty-day stint in rehab, I purchased a minivan so that I could transport her home to Jasper, Georgia, in comfort. This woman sacrificed her whole life to raise not only her four natural children but also, in her later years, the four young children of her sister, who'd passed away from cancer, when she married her brother-in-law. That's correct. My uncle became my stepfather, and my cousins became my half brothers and sisters. She was a saint among saints.

I worked my ass off in my earlier years, I had the means, and I was going to spoil my mother in the remaining years she had left. I had Kanyon purchase her the most comfortable adjustable bed you could buy. I used to carry Mom up two flights of stairs to give her a bath, so I installed a walk-in tub in her closet in her ground floor bedroom suite. I hired her a private nurse.

This nurse, named Kathy, had the biggest heart but was the dumbest hillbilly, white trash, beer-drinking, pontoon boat, tobacco-chewing redneck you had ever met in your life. I affectionately called her Dumbass. She was a chronic cigarette smoker, and we got off to one hell of a rough start. I actually fired her the first night because she hacked all night, keeping Mom awake. But we eventually became great friends and kept mom in stitches with our comic routine, cussing at each other all day about how stupid the other was. We just adored each other. When Mom passed away, I felt sorrier for Kathy than anyone else. Mom had become Kathy's baby. Kathy was just lost.

Well, we just had an absolute blast over the next three years. And interestingly enough, Mom never asked about her husband, Tony, which solved a great problem. And on the very few occasions that she asked about Robert, we told her he was in jail for drugs, as she knew of his problems; and that was that. We always used to joke about what it would be like when she passed away and ran into them in heaven and said, "What the heck are you doing up here?" Laugh out loud.

Over the next three years, we spoiled mom as much as we could. Tony, her husband of thirty years, never took Mom anywhere not even out to dinner. We took Mom to the Virgin Islands, the Florida Keys, and Disney World; treated her to fine dining; visited parks;

and so on. She had a grand time. Mom ate steaks and lobsters and went to the theater.

My wife and kids loved her like their own. I could not have been more grateful to those who loved and cared for her. All that she missed out in her lifetime we squeezed into her last three years.

One particular morning, Kathy was off, and I was on duty. I took Mom to the bathroom as usual about 6:00 a.m. I put Mom back in bed. About 9:00 a.m., I came in and asked if she was ready to get up for the day. Mom stated she had a headache. I gave her two Tylenol and told her I would come back in thirty minutes. When I was getting ready to leave the room, she reached out for my hand. I knelt by her side, and her light left her tired eyes. She suffered a massive life-ending stroke in my arms. I knew exactly what was happening. I held Mom in my arms, stroking her hair and telling her it was OK. "Go join your Tony. I love you. And I will see you again."

These past three and a half years were the greatest privilege of my life.

34
CHAPTER

◆

Mom

WHEN MOTHER PASSED, WE RECEIVED AN OUTPOURING of flowers, gifts, and food. The most important treasure I have and what is dear to my heart is a sympathy card presented to me by my stepmother, Christy. This card was authored by Amy Abernathy Designer as a tribute to her mother, Tammy, who had recently passed.

It reads as follows:

I'm sure you'll miss her.

The very one who rocked you in the beginning needed you most in the end.

You were there with your tender heart and your steadfast loyalty, doing the right thing, exactly the way she had hoped, exactly the way she taught you to do so.

35
CHAPTER

◆

Short Journey

T O SAY THIS FIVE-DAY JOURNEY HAS BEEN BIZARRE IS AN understatement. At any given moment, I await Rod Sterling and Allen Funt to say, "You're on *Candid Camera*." This experience was never about saving Brayly's life. Bre was always going to be fine. Bre's event, although horrific, was nothing more than a vehicle that opened doors in my brain that I never knew existed—and the ability for me to reach a potential, if only for five short days, that I never even knew I had. It enabled me to think just a little bit more out of the box.

I'm not going to lie to you. Physically, I love this burst of energy. Mentally, I hate the person I've become. I've hurt each and every member of my family more than I can bear. I want the old boring Gunmolly back. I enjoyed the vacation, but I want to come back home. If my memoir, in some infinite way, helps prevent or mend the agony of anyone, then the mental torture I've endured for the past fifteen years will have been so very well worth it. This short journey has been orchestrated by a power greater than I will ever understand.

I've made an appointment with the Amen Clinic not only for Bre but also for myself. Hopefully they can learn and educate others about the phenomenon that has occurred here in less than twelve hours. Something, for whatever reason, has opened a door in my brain that I hope closes soon. As exciting as it is to have a purpose, this scares the hell out of me, as well as anyone who is unfortunate enough to cross my path. I don't know why. But for some reason, someone or something needs this story to be told. I have the energy of an eighteen-year-old on an eight ball of cocaine and haven't slept more than an hour a night for the past three weeks, and I'm constantly refreshed.

I've never questioned my faith, and I've always believed in fate. Having never experienced fate, three incidents in the last three months have presented themselves to me that bear recognition. Two were mind-blowing and very encouraging, while the last, but not in that order, was devastating.

Remember earlier when Damian was having a heart attack every day for about three months? (Cracks me up thinking about it. Any who!) After spending my entire retirement fund on tests you would generally see performed on an eighty-year-old—stress tests echocardiograms, and the like—he was told he was a perfectly healthy, grossly obese teen with halitosis.

I decided this kid needed a psychiatrist. Being nineteen and an adult, Damian went on his own. I asked him how his $500 session went, and apparently, he and the therapist flirted the entire session and exchanged sexual escapades. That's not entirely true. She did tell him he had self-esteem problems. I wonder where he got that from? I apologize. I needed a moment of sanity before I got back to the lunacy that has now occupied my brain for forty-seven hours.

Let's get back to fate. Do you remember earlier when I mentioned Sue, the cognitive behavioral therapist and massage therapist who told me about the Amen Clinic? Just keep remembering the Amen Clinic. Briefly, what they do is this: Over the past thirty years, with the world's largest database of brain scans, they utilize a brain-based process that helps us find the root causes of PTSD, depression, anxiety, addiction, or memory issues. Having experience with over 160,000 brain SPECT scans, they evaluate the brain's blood flow. The emphasis is on maximizing your brain's potential through diagnosis and then treatment.

36

CHAPTER

◆

Fate Incident Number Two

MY WIFE IS A HIGH SCHOOL ENGLISH LITERATURE TEACHER and, as I mentioned earlier, head cheer coach. Two years ago, she was named teacher of the year for Pickens County, Georgia. To say I'm proud of my Kanyon is an understatement. I believe the layperson thinks a career in education is an easy seven-to-three job. It could not be farther from the truth. My wife leaves the house at 6:30 a.m. and, with cheer practice, gets home about 6:00 p.m. Monday through Friday. Once home, Kanyon changes into her jammies—or they could be her great-grandmother's; they are equally sexy—and then delves into grading papers and preparing lesson plans. It's the same story on the weekends. Kanyon easily puts in seventy hours each and every week.

"B-B-B-But teachers have the summers off."

I call *bullshit*. She has dead week. That is the week of the Fourth of July off, and that is it—period. The rest of the summer is cheer camps, both sideline and competition.

I put my foot down about a month ago and told Kanyon we need to enjoy our summers. We agreed to buy a motor home. I started my search and found a possibility.

The seller was like my brother from another mother. In our three-hour, let's-become-best-friends convo I told him about my daughter's medical problems. Get ready for this. Grab ya popcorn. He pulled out his wife's business card and told me I needed to contact his wife, Nadine Psareas. Are you ready? Nadine is the director of the Amen Clinic in Atlanta. *You can't make this shit up!*

I about fell of the roof of the motorhome. Can you seriously tell me a higher power isn't at work here?

The third and last fate-related incident isn't so palatable. In an effort to make things easier for Kanyon upon my demise, I prepurchased our funeral arrangements. We both wanted to be in coffins, but I didn't want to be underneath six feet of earth. So I bought a crypt for Kanyon and me. This served three purposes. One, we were both in coffins. Two, I could get out easier when I needed to (LOL). But most importantly, three, we could enjoy the perpetual smell of McDonald's French fries grease because there was one right across the street.

Little did I know—and I found out many years later—this greatly upset the children, specifically Brayly. I had no idea. I went to the funeral home and asked if I could horse trade (we do that here in the South) my $12,000 luxurious, marble, third-row-from-the ground, climate-controlled crypt for a piece of dirt. They were quite eager. But in order to do an even swap because the funeral home did not want to refund any money, I had to swap nine plots in a row.

I thought to myself, *What the hell am I going to do with nine plots? There are only four of us. Sublet out the other five?*

Problem solved. We are adopting quintuplets from Chapultepec.

Back to the eerie part. I was excited to show Brayly our trade, and the first words out of her mouth were—and I quote—"I know what color coffin I want, and I already have my dress picked out!"

WTF!

37
CHAPTER

◆

What is Cooking in My Brain?

I F IT'S MY TURN AND SOMETHING IS CHANGING IN MY BRAIN OR my health that has allowed me to come to the aid of others, I will embrace my destiny openheartedly. If it's my turn to join my lost loved ones, I will rejoice with them and gaze down on those I've left behind, admiring the love of my life, Kanyon; my children; Amanda and her oh-so-sweet life partner, Tori; and my son, Damian. I will pray for them nightly and beg God to be merciful in their transition as I wait for them in heaven.

Brayly's seizures were incorrectly diagnosed by every Doctor we took her to. I gave up sleeping for 4 weeks surfing the web to find the answers. This loss of sleep and losing 58Lbs in 7 weeks sent me into another psychotic break but I and I alone found the cause of Brayly's seizures and saved her life. Brayly was hit with what I call the perfect storm. Her immune system was compromised because she was recovering from Covid 19. The two back to back concussions opened the door in her brain for seizure activity but the most important thing I discovered was Brayly's diet. Her typical teenage diet of biscuits and sweet tea for breakfast, chicken tenders fries and sweet tea for lunch and dinner caused the seizures. It is documented that sugar and wheat are linked to seizures. I put Brayly on a Keto diet and within 3 weeks she went from 3 seizures a day to zero. Brayly has been seizure free for months now. The doctor and psychiatrists diagnosed her with Psychogenic nonepileptic seizures. This is a bull shit diagnosis (Although a very horrific condition) they pegged my daughter with because they did not spend the time to properly diagnose her. I did, went insane doing it, and saved her life because their diagnosis made her suicidal.

When I wrote the book in those manic 12 hours. I knew this was my story but I was simply a vehicle through which a higher power was telling this story. I predicted that something was wrong in my brain 2 months before my brain was scanned at the Amen Clinic. My brain scan revealed a lesion in the pre-frontal cortex of my brain. My doctor diagnosed me with Hypomania and told me this lesion allowed me to tap into other areas of my brain not regularily used. A good analogy would be a person who has never picked up a paint brush out of nowhere can suddenly paint like Picasso. These lesions are extremely rare. With God's grace my lesion is non-cancerous and with medication I have returned to the Vince my family knows and adores. I will never write again.

AUTHOR'S ATTESTATION

I know a good deal of the meat in this shit sandwich life of mine is a hard pill to swallow. That being said, I just wanted to thank you, my readers, for taking the time out of your busy day to read my memoir. I attest, on all that is sacred and holy, that each and every word, statement, and illustration is true, so help me God!

Very Gratefully,
Gunmolly Kodiad

Printed in the United States
by Baker & Taylor Publisher Services